THE YOUNG ENTREPRENEURS FINANCIAL LITERACY HANDBOOK PERSONAL FINANCE

DEBORAH REYNOLDS

PUBLISHER: CREDIBLE MATH

Author: Deborah Reynolds

Photo Images: iStockphoto.com

Any internet websites printed are used as resources only.
The mention of these websites should not be considered an endorsement by the author or
Credible Math, LLC and we do not vouch for the content of these websites over the life of this book.

Copyright: 2012 by Deborah Reynolds. Revised 2nd Edition: 2023. All rights reserved.

No part of this book may be reproduced or transmitted in any form or by any means, mechanical, electronic, including recording and photocopying, or by any information storage or retrieval system, without the prior written approval of Deborah Reynolds unless such copying is expressly permitted by federal copyright law. Address all inquiries to Deborah Reynolds, 20 Baltimore Ave., Piscataway, New Jersey 08854.

CONTENTS

Topic 1. Mo Money, Mo Money, Mo Money 1

Topic 2. Shop Till You Drop 9

Topic 3. Dreams Versus Goals and Budgets 15

Topic 4. The World of Banking and Investing 21

Topic 5. The Importance of Credit 31

Topic 6. Famous Entrpreneurs and Ceos 37

Answer Key 41

About the Author and Credible Math 47

TOPIC 1
MO MONEY, MO MONEY, MO MONEY

OBJECTIVES

If you want to become rich you should be able to:

- Identify and represent different money denominations
- Count money using as few coins and bills as possible
- Read and write numbers using dollars and cents
- Understand the purpose of money and how it affects the economy?
- Investigate cryptocurrency and what distinguishes it from other money denominations. State why it has become widely used and valuable.

WARM-UP

- What is your money IQ?

- What are the Benjamins?

- What are "Dead Presidents"?

- Before money, what system was used to pay for goods and services?

- Which government agency controls the amount of money available for use in the United States?

- What is digital currency or cryptocurrency? What are some of the most popular?

LESSON HIGHLIGHTS

Before money, people bartered or traded to obtain any goods or services they needed. For example an auto mechanic may fix an accountants car in exchange for getting his income tax return prepared. This barter system is still used today by a few people.

Today coins and bills are used because a standard unit of value is needed. They are also easier to carry. Coins are no longer made of all copper or silver metal, but rather a combination of copper and nickel. Coin denominations and values are the penny (1cent), nickel (5 cents), dime (10 cents), quarter (25 cents), half-dollar (50 cents), and dollar (100 cents). The bills or paper money denominations are $1, $2, $5, $10, $20, $50, and $100.

Paper money is also called Federal Reserve notes. The Federal Reserve is a government agency which controls the supply of money and rates.

The actions of the Federal Reserve can have an impact on the management of resources or the economy of the United States and the world.

The Federal Reserve can raise or lower prime lending rates. These are the best interest rates (lowest rates) that banks use when determining interest rates on credit cards, mortgages, car loans, and personal loans. People with the highest credit scores (higher than 750 get the lowest rates. People with poor credit scores (lower than 650) who don't pay their bills on time get higher interest rates. They will pay more to borrow the same amount of money. The Federal Reserve raises interest rates to control inflation or prevent the costs of goods and services from going up and stop unemployment. Inflation impacts not only citizens in the United States but also around the world(globally).

Cryptocurrency is digital currency on the internet used to buy goods and services. It is also used as an investment in the stock market. This currency is decentralized or not controlled by the government. To keep track of all transactions a technology called a blockchain is used to keep transactions secure. The blockchain acts as a balance sheet. Because it is not controlled by the government, illegal transactions have occurred.

Cryptocurrency was first introduced in 2008 with Bitcoin which is still the largest and most expensive. Other cryptocurrencies are Ethereum, Litecoin, Tezos, and Bitcoin Cash. Cryptocurrency can be purchased at online exchanges such as Coinbase.

ACTIVITY

Complete the following chart using real or fake money. You may also research the answers using the internet. The first column lists the various monetary denominations. Looking at both sides identify the famous person on one side and the famous place or symbol on the other side.

Denomination	Famous Person	Famous Place/Symbol
Penny		
Nickel		
Dime		
Quarter		
Half-Dollar		
Silver Dollar		
$1		
$2		
$5		
$10		
$20		
$50		
$100		

ACTIVITY

Answer each question below and tell how many of each type of money denomination would represent your answer using the least number of coins and bills.

1. Write twelve hundred fifty eight dollars and sixty nine cents using the dollar sign and a decimal point.

Pennies	Nickels	Dimes	Quarters	$1	$5	$10	$20	$100

2. Kevin purchased five games for $29.99 each plus an additional tax of 7%. He gave the cashier two hundred dollar bills. How much change did he get back?

Pennies	Nickels	Dimes	Quarters	$1	$5	$10	$20	$100

NEXT MEETING

Select five items to buy at the mall. Bring pictures and prices. If coupons are available bring those also.

_____
_____
_____
_____
_____
_____
_____
_____
_____
_____

TOPIC 2
SHOP TILL YOU DROP

OBJECTIVES

If you want to accumulate wealth you should be able to:

- Distinguish between wants and needs.
- Calculate unit price to determine the best deal
- Compare regular price and sales price
- List advantages and disadvantages of cash purchases versus credit card purchases.

WARM-UP

Write below five items on your shopping list and check whether they are a want or need.

SHOPPING LIST

	ITEM	WANT	NEED
1			
2			
3			
4			
5			

LESSON HIGHLIGHTS

Money is a tool which allows us to obtain the things we need. We can buy food, clothing, cars, and homes. We can buy the latest technology in computers, phones, and games. We can take vacations and eat in restaurants. Money allows us to become independent and not depend on others to supply our needs. Money allows us to have more self-esteem.

No matter how much money we make, we should always control the amount we spend. To accumulate wealth we must always spend less than we make and make wise purchases. We should distinguish between wants and needs, and refrain from too much impulsive spending.

We should also look for sales and use coupons to reduce the items regular or original price. When purchasing food, it is wise to buy in bulk, or more than one of each item. Large warehouse outlets such as Costco, BJ's and Sam's Club are popular places for buying in bulk. They package items such as ketchup and toothpaste with two or three in a package. The package usually shows the unit price (price of one) and total price.

When shopping we can pay using cash, debit card, or credit card. Cash is usually best, but many times credit cards are used when you don't have cash or a debit card.

A credit card is a type of bank loan. You can make a purchase today and pay later. However if you do not pay the purchase amount within thirty days the bank will charge you an additional amount called **interest**. Thus a $300 television set bought using a credit card could end up costing you much more depending on the interest rate and the length of time you take paying off the credit card.

1. Complete the following table and calculate the unit price (price of one unit of measure).

    Unit price = Price ÷ Number of Units

Item & Size	Price	Unit Price
Ketchup A – 40 oz.	$4.10	Per oz.
Ketchup B – 12 0z.	$2.38	Per oz.

Which ketchup is the best deal?

2. Macy's is having a special sale on Wednesday and will reduce the price of ladies and men watches. A Michael Kors watch that regularly sales for $360 will be reduced by 15%. What will be the sales price before tax is added?

NEXT MEETING

1. Write something you dream of having or doing.
   _____
   _____
   _____
   _____
   _____

2. Write something you would like to accomplish or get within a year.
   _____
   _____
   _____
   _____
   _____

TOPIC 3
DREAMS VERSUS GOALS AND BUDGETS

OBJECTIVES

A successful business owner should be able to:

- Develop short and long-term goals
- Distinguish income from expense items
- Prepare a budget

WARM-UP

1. Write something you dream of having or doing.

2. Write a career goal.

LESSON HIGHLIGHTS

Goals are objectives that we work towards achieving. They may be **short-term goals** which can be achieved in less than three months. Examples are exercise 20 minutes daily for a month; save money for an upcoming concert ticket; and increase store sales 10% over last month's sales.

Intermediate goals are those which can be achieved within 3 months to a year. Saving for a car down payment or a new computer is an intermediate goal. **Long-term goals** take longer than a year to achieve. Purchasing a home or business is a long-term goal.

No matter what type of goal you set, they should be **SMART** (specific, measurable, attainable, realistic, and timely).

To achieve a goal it is important to create and write a personal goal statement. This statement helps you understand what the goal is about and why it is important to you.

This process helps you select a time frame and keep focused.

BUDGETS

To achieve our financial goals it is important that we prepare a **budget** which serves as the foundation of any financial plan.

A **budget** is a financial statement written for a future period of time. It shows your **income/revenue** (where your money comes from) or how much you have and your **expenses** (where your money goes). A budget shows the best way to distribute these funds.

Personal budgets are very important because they help us keep personal spending under control and allow us to save and reach short term and long term goals. The importance of a budget should be taught at an early age when children start receiving an allowance. Managing money becomes a habit and easily translates into becoming an adult managing a business budget. The following page is an example of a personal monthly budget. It lists all the names and amounts of money coming into the home each month and the names and amounts of money or expenses that must be paid out each month. By preparing a budget one can make the necessary adjustments so that the expenses are always less than the income.

Personal Monthly Budget

	Month_____ Year
INCOME	
Wages/Tips	$ 5,280.00
Interest income	$ 2.00
Other Income	$ 250.00
Total Income	$ 5,532.00
EXPENSES:	
Savings	$ 200.00
Rent/Mortgage	$ 1,670.00
Health Insurance	$ 320.00
Car Payment	$ 360.00
Car Insurance	$ 225.00

Utilities	$ 230.00
Phone	$ 146.00
Cable	$ 87.00
Credit Cards/Store Accounts	$ 180.00
School Loans	$ 260.00
Groceries	$ 400.00
Transportation/Gas	$ 230.00
Laundry/Cleaners	$ 128.00
Clothing/Hair Allowance	$ 225.00
Entertainment	$ 240.00
Gifts	$ 5.00
Other Expenses	$ 200.00
Total Expenses	$ 5,106.00
NET INCOME	$ 426.00

In the chart below place the dollar amount of each item in either the income or expense column. When completed calculate the total for the income and total for the expenses.

	ITEM	INCOME	EXPENSE
1	Allowance $100/month		
2	Cell phone $95/month		
3	Payroll check $2600/month		
4	Rent $850/month		
5	Cable and internet $193/month		
	TOTALS		

What is the **net income** (income – expenses)? _____

Help your parents prepare a monthly budget using the following chart.

BUDGET FOR MONTH OF_____

INCOME	AMOUNT
WAGES/TIPS	
INTEREST INCOME	
OTHER INCOME	
TOTAL INCOME	
EXPENSES	
SAVINGS	
RENT/MORTGAGE	
GAS, ELECTRIC, & CABLE	
CAR PAYMENT & TRANSPORTATION	
HEALTH INSURANCE & AUTO INSURANCE	
CABLE	
CREDIT CARDS	
GROCERIES	
CLOTHING/HAIR/ENTERTAINMENT	
OTHER EXPENSES	
TOTAL EXPENSES	
NET INCOME	

Topic 4
THE WORLD OF BANKING AND INVESTING

OBJECTIVES

In order to reach your financial goals and acquire wealth you should:

- Establish a relationship with a bank by maintaining an account.
- Become familiar with the different types of accounts and services offered by banks.
- Explain the different types of investment vehicles.
- Learn how to read stock quotations ticker tape.

WARM-UP

Why is a budget important when setting financial goals?
_____
_____
_____
_____
_____

LESSON HIGHLIGHTS

BANKS PURPOSE

Banks are institutions established for the purpose of holding money for individuals, corporations, and governments. They pay interest for the use of this money. They also loan money to other individuals, corporations, and governments at a higher rate of interest than they pay in order to make a profit. Banks also invest this money in securities (stocks and bonds).

BANKING SERVICES

Banks today offer services for all your financial transactions. They offer a variety of checking, savings, credit cards, and investment accounts.

Checking accounts enable you to write checks as a form of payment based on the amount of money you have in your account. This account also allows you to use an automatic teller machine (ATM). There are different types of checking accounts some of which pay a small amount of interest.

Savings accounts usually require a minimum balance. Sometimes savings accounts are linked to checking accounts to make it easier to transfer money between the two accounts. The interest the bank pays you for this account varies from bank to bank. Therefore it is good to shop around for the best rate.

INTEREST

Interest is the cost of using or borrowing money. It is the amount the bank pays you for the use of your money or charges you for lending you money. The amount depends on a rate or percentage which is tied to the prime interest rate tied to the financial markets and the Federal Reserve Bank.

Interest = Principal x Rate x Time

Example: Calculate the interest paid on a $12,000 loan at 5% for 4 years.

Answer: Interest = 12,000 x .05 x4 = $2,400.00

ONLINE BANKING

Online banking provides the ability to do 24-hour banking using the internet and various electronic devices. It is sometimes called home banking or web banking. Customers can check bank balances; pay bills; transfer money between accounts; apply for mortgages; and use direct deposit to have payroll checks deposited into our account.

PAYMENT NETWORKS

Over the past several years banks have created apps for customers to quickly send and receive money from their bank account to someone else's bank account. Zelle, PayPal, Venmo, Cash App, Apple Pay, and Google Pay are some of the more popular apps.

INVESTMENTS

To i**nvest** money is to commit money for future **gain** or profit. We commit money to **securities** or accounts which are secured by assets. The three most common types of securities are **stocks**, **bonds**, and **certificates of deposit**. These assets are usually represented by partial ownership in a company or corporation. You hope the value of these securities will increase over time.

The money you invest in a corporation allows it to grow and operate more effectively. When you purchase shares of stock, you become a **stockholder** or **shareholder**. The price of a share of stock may change from day to day. You can keep track of the price by reading the newspaper, using the internet, or watching the business channel. Remember when you purchase a share of Nike or Apple stock; you become an owner in the company. Stocks are purchased through brokerage houses such as Charles Schwab, Fidelity, Merrill, JP Morgan,

E*Trade (Morgan Stanley), Robinhood, and SoFi. The price of stock is reported daily on exchanges such as the New York Stock Exchange (NYSE). Buying stocks, bonds, or certificates should be viewed as long term investments. Because the price of a share of stock can sometimes be costly, some investment companies like SoFi, allow you to purchase partial shares.

EXCHANGE-TRADED FUND (ETF)

ETFs are a new method to buy and sell stock. They allow you to bundle several stocks and thus diversify your portfolio and lessen losses. However, when you buy an ETF, you are not buying a stock share.

NON-FUNGIBLE TOKENS (NFT)

NFTs are like cryptocurrencies such as Bitcoin because they are generated using the same programming and blockchain technology. The owner of the NFT can say they have the original. It's like owning an original piece of art. The owner hopes that over time its value will increase. Art, music, and even some high school athletes have NFTs.

ACTIVITIES

1. Pick two stocks from the newspaper, and in the boxes below write the names of the stocks; the fifty-two week low and high price; the previous day closing price, the one day change, one year change, and year to date (YTD) percent change.

NAME	52 WEEK LOW	52 WEEK HIGH	CLOSING PRICE	1 DAY CHANGE	1 YEAR CHANGE	YTD % CHANGE

NEXT MEETING

Research the names of different credit cards and banks issuing these cards.

TOPIC 5
THE IMPORTANCE OF CREDIT

OBJECTIVES

Before obtaining credit, you should:

- Explain how credit affects your personal and business finances
- Identify the three Cs of credit.
- Explain the advantages and disadvantages of buying on credit
- Determine the long-term effect of good and bad credit.

WARM-UP

1. James borrowed $13,000 to purchase a car. He paid off the loan in five years. At the end of five years he had paid the bank $14,630. How much interest did he pay?

_____
_____
_____
_____
_____

LESSON HIGHLIGHTS

Credit has many definitions. Credit is confidence in a buyer's or borrower's ability to pay their financial obligations. It can be an arrangement for a person or business to buy goods now and pay later. Credit is the amount placed by a bank at a borrower's disposal. Credit is also payment made on a loan to reduce the amount owed on the loan. All these definitions affect the way we achieve personal goals and business success.

When determining who is eligible for credit, one formula known as the **three Cs of credit** is used:

1. Character – Does the borrower have an honest reputation?
2. Capacity – Based on borrower's income and expenses, can the borrower repay?
3. Capital – What are the borrower's physical and financial assets or collateral?

Good credit will help you obtain a college education, a car loan, a home mortgage, and money to grow a business. Good credit allows you to book hotels and rent cars when taking vacations. Most sales over the internet are done using credit cards. Good credit allows you to enjoy a good life and pay much less interest than someone with poor credit.

Remember that credit is a loan that must be repaid on time. By not paying these loans on time and having too many credit cards you stand the risk of getting a low or poor credit score. Your credit score affects most things you want to do financially. It may even affect your ability to get a job. Bad credit can also lead to unwanted stress and poor health.

ACTIVITY

Write three conclusions that can be drawn from information presented in this lesson.

1. _____

2. _____

3. _____

NEXT MEETING

Research a famous entrepreneur or chief executive officer and write about their achievements and company. Be prepared make an oral presentation.

_____
_____
_____
_____
_____
_____
_____
_____
_____
_____
_____

TOPIC 6
FAMOUS ENTRPRENEURS AND CEOS

OBJECTIVE

In order to succeed in business, you should:

- Research and study the lives of successful entrepreneurs and chief executive officers (CEOs).

WARM-UP

Why is it more advantageous to own a share of Nike stock than buy a pair of expensive Nike sneakers?

LESSON HIGHLIGHTS

An **entrepreneur** is a person who creates, organizes, operates, and owns a business. They assume the financial risk and responsibilities in starting and running a new business or **venture**. **Entrepreneurship** is the process of identifying a potential business, finding and testing it on potential customers, and obtaining the financing to start the business.

To help develop new business opportunities, you must identify current business trends. The biggest trends today are e-business and e-commerce which use the internet. Almost every field including retail sales, education, finance, and publishing do business on the internet. Service businesses such as fitness centers, pet grooming, food catering, and wedding planning are on the rise. Green (environmental) and home-based businesses are also increasing. As a young entrepreneur you would like to connect to all of these trends.

Many new entrepreneurs choose **franchising** when starting their own business. When you purchase a franchise, you become the owner of an outpost of a larger corporation. McDonalds, Burger King, Midas, Stanley Steamer, and Comfort Inn are examples of franchise businesses. When purchasing a franchise you purchase a territory and franchisor's business system, which includes accounting, advertising, and operational procedures.

If we look at the lives of some famous entrepreneurs such as Oprah Winfrey (OWN), Mark Zuckerberg (Meta/ Facebook) Tyler Perry (Tyler Perry Studios), Elon Musk (Tesla), Rihanna (Fenty), Jeff Bezos (Amazon), and Bernard Arnault and family (LVMH/Louis Vuitton, Dior, and Tiffany), we find that their environments and interest provided the inspiration for their success.

A number of minorities and women have also made great advancements as leaders in the business world by becoming chief executive officers of large corporations. Thasunda Brown Duckett (Chase Consumer Banking), Marvin Ellison (Lowe's Company), Roz Brewer (Walgreens), and Oscar Munoz (United Airlines), are just a few.

ACTIVITY

Students research famous entrepreneurs and chief operating officers using the internet or library and write a short report. Students should also orally present their findings to the class.

Answer Key

MO MONEY, MO MONEY, MO MONEY

WARM-UP: WHAT IS YOUR MONEY IQ?

1. What are the Benjamins? $100 dollar bills
2. What are "Dead Presidents"? US paper money
3. Before money, what system was used to pay for goods and services? Barter system
4. Which government agency controls the amount of money

ACTIVITY

Complete the following chart using real or fake money. You may also research the answers using the internet. The first column lists the various monetary denominations. Looking at both sides identify the famous person on one side and the famous place or symbol on the other side.

Denomination	Famous Person	Famous Place/Symbol
Penny	Abraham Lincoln	Lincoln Memorial
Nickel	Thomas Jefferson	Monticello
Dime	Franklin Roosevelt	Torch &laurel/oak sprigs
Quarter	George Washington	Eagle
Half-Dollar	John F. Kennedy	Presidential Seal
Silver Dollar	Susan B. Anthony	Eagle
$1	George Washington	The Great Seal
$2	Thomas Jefferson	Signing of the Declaration of Independence
$5	Abraham Lincoln	Lincoln Memorial
$10	Alexander Hamilton	US Treasury
$20	Andrew Jackson	The White House
$50	Ulysses S. Grant	US Capitol
$100	Benjamin Franklin	Independence Hall

1. Write four hundred thirty-two dollars and forty-five cents using the dollar sign and a decimal point. $432.45

Pennies	Nickels	Dimes	Quarters	$1	$5	$10	$20	$100
		2	1	2		1	1	4

2. Kevin purchased a game for $29.99 plus an additional tax of $2.08. He gave the cashier two twenty-dollar bills. How much change did he get back? $7.93

Pennies	Nickels	Dimes	Quarters	$1	$5	$10	$20	$100
3	1	1	3	2	1			

3. Macy's is having a special sale on Wednesday and will reduce the price of ladies and men watches. A Michael Kors watch that regularly sales for $360 will be reduced by $70. What will be the sales price before tax is added? $290.00

SHOP TILL YOU DROP

1. Complete the following table and calculate the unit price (price of one unit of measure).

Unit price = Price ÷ Number of Units

Item & Size	Price	Unit Price
Ketchup A -40 oz.	$4.20	$0.11 Per oz.
Ketchup B – 12 Oz.	$2.40	$0.20 Per oz.

Which ketchup is the best deal? Ketchup A

DREAMS VERSUS GOALS AND BUDGETS

In the chart below place the dollar amount of each item in either the income or expense column. When completed calculate the total for the income and total for the expenses.

	ITEM	INCOME	EXPENSE
1	Allowance $100/month	$100	
2	Cell phone $95/month		$95
3	Payroll check $2600/month	2600	
4	Rent $850/month		850
5	Cable and internet $193/month		193
	TOTALS	$2700	$1138

What is the **net income** (income – expenses)? $1562

CREDIBLE MATH, LLC

Specializing in Financial Literacy, Entrepreneurship, & Workplace Readiness Programs

ABOUT THE AUTHOR AND CREDIBLE MATH

Credible Math is a company dedicated to advancing the educational achievements of students in mathematics and financial literacy through curriculum development and teacher support.

Deborah Reynolds is an experienced mathematics educator who has taught high school mathematics and written math curriculum in Plainfield, New Jersey for twenty- five years. Prior to coming to Plainfield, she worked as an assistant treasurer/controller for a major New York bank and as a mathematician for a major aircraft engine corporation outside Cincinnati, Ohio. She began her professional career as a high school mathematics teacher for the Pittsburgh Pennsylvania Public School System.

She is currently an educational consultant helping schools and community organizations develop financial literacy programs. In addition, she is a workshop presenter whose topics are "Introduction to the Stock Market and Online Stock Trading" and "How To Write A Book, From An Idea To A Reality".

Mrs. Reynolds holds a B.S. degree in mathematics from Duquesne University and a Ms. Ed in mathematics from the University of Pittsburgh.

www.ingramcontent.com/pod-product-compliance
Lightning Source LLC
Chambersburg PA
CBHW061146010526
44118CB00026B/2888